MW00592785

THE PEANUT PRINCIPLE

GIVING VOICE TO THE SPIRIT WITHIN YOU

AURELIA PALCHER

FERNE PRESS

The Peanut Principle: Giving Voice to the Spirit within You
Copyright © 2011 by Aurelia Palcher
Layout and cover design by Kimberly Franzen and Raphael Giuffrida.
Printed in Canada

Summary: An observation of the many ways we confuse and confound ourselves in our quest for a balanced, fulfilled life, and the methods we can use to regain that balance and fulfillment.

Library of Congress Cataloging-in-Publication Data
   Palcher, Aurelia
   The Peanut Principle: Giving Voice to the Spirit within You /
   Aurelia Palcher – First Edition
   ISBN-13: 978-1-933916-86-6
     1. Healthy lifestyles. 2. Fulfillment.
   I. Palcher, Aurelia II. Title
   Library of Congress Control Number: 2011925627

Manufactured by Friesens Corporation
in Altona, Manitoba, March 2011
Docket 64854

FERNE PRESS

Ferne Press is an imprint of Nelson Publishing & Marketing
366 Welch Road, Northville, MI 48167
www.nelsonpublishingandmarketing.com
(248) 735-0418

I am deeply grateful to the many people who shared their personal experiences that in turn provided the reflections for this book. I am also grateful for all those who provided support during the development of this book—especially to John for his endless patience.

INTRODUCTION

The last time I went to the circus, we arrived early so we could observe the activities taking place prior to the show. The main attraction was the opportunity to take an elephant ride, and the crowd responded enthusiastically. Group after group of people climbed up to the brace on the back of the elephant for the thrill of a ride, and the elephant continually submitted to the command to go around in circles to provide this thrill. Occasionally the trainer threw some peanuts to keep the elephant going. But that is precisely what happened—it kept going round and round in the same circle. It was like a robot, performing a task but devoid of a spirit within. I am still haunted by this image and the emptiness in the eyes of that elephant as it was dragged down by the weight of the people riding on its back.

This image of the elephant becomes even more haunting to me with the realization that we likewise engage in such behavior. The most basic and universal search of humankind is related to the search for personal identity and purpose. Such questions as "Who am I?" and "What is my purpose in being here?" reflect a desire to connect with our inner self in order that we may find meaning. It is a search for integrity in the way we live and implies some kind of disconnect from our authentic inner self. But connecting to this inner spirit is not an easy process. It is a *discovery* as well as a *recovery* process. It is a discovery in that it requires us to identify the ways in which we have invalidly defined who we are, and it is a recovery in that we must disentangle ourselves from the behaviors that may have unintentionally kept our spirit bound up within. Unless we are aware of how this dynamic is present in our lives, we may become victims of our own choices and lose, rather than possess, the power of who we are. Ultimately we may not even recognize that we are living in a false relationship with ourselves.

The process can be likened to the conditioning process of the circus elephant. The elephant is a magnificent animal in its natural environment. It is the largest and most powerful animal in the jungle and at the same time exhibits very sensitive behavior. It belongs to a strong social unit that manifests great care for its young and old. It is emotionally complex and has been observed to shed tears at the death of another elephant. In its natural habitat it is unencumbered as it exhibits these qualities that authentically characterize the elephant. Because it is in possession of its own power, there is a congruency between what it is and what it does. But when the determination is made that the elephant will perform in the circus, these natural qualities are sacrificed.

It is safe to assume that no elephant ever has the goal of performing in a circus. It becomes a circus performer because that is the goal of the trainer. It is clearly in the best interest of the circus—not the elephant. The job of the trainer, therefore, is to manipulate the elephant so that it will eventually view performing in the circus as not only acceptable but even desirable. This complex conditioning process is eventually accomplished because of the rewards that are provided. And it is in the very process of accepting these rewards that the elephant loses its sense of self. The elephant is rewarded for subjecting itself to the commands of the trainer, who is redefining it for the trainer's own use. It is being transformed into a commodity for the entertainment of the circus audience. Even though it is innocent and unsuspecting, this does not change the result—the elephant becomes victim to the power that another holds over it. Initially some rather sophisticated conditioning techniques are used, but eventually the elephant is rewarded with mere peanuts. It is almost unbelievable to realize that the power of this magnificent animal is so vulnerable that ultimately it can be sacrificed for the reward of a peanut! But this happens because of the seductive nature of rewards. They are presented and perceived as positive rather than negative. The elephant accepts the peanuts as a reward for the behavior that pleases the trainer. In doing so, externally it remains an elephant, but essentially this is just an empty shell because its spirit has been suppressed. The magnificent qualities that energized the spirit of the elephant have been covered up by artificial characteristics that mold it into a predetermined pattern. In fact, that is the very point of the whole process. The circus elephant is pleasing to the audience because it does what an elephant is not supposed to do. It amuses the crowds by standing on stools and performing other cute little tricks precisely because these things are contrary to the nature of the elephant. Its weakness rather than its power is showcased. It is rewarded not for what it is but for how it will perform. In a sense it becomes the peanuts it eats. Some may argue that a circus elephant has gained many more comforts than an elephant in the jungle. But we may also ask if any comfort is worth sacrificing one's very soul.

We, too, are seduced by the reward that peanuts offer and become oblivious to the fact that they actually diminish the power within us. Because the process is so subtle, we may even believe that what we are doing is right and good. We may do it to "make someone else happy," "fit in," "look good," or "get ahead," but uninformed choices still result in unintended consequences. When we relinquish the power to be true to who we are, we become victims of exploitation. We become like the elephant that performs for the crowd without regard for our own authentic self.

The purpose of this book is to develop an awareness of such "elephant" behavior in our lives so we can identify how such peanuts can threaten the integrity of who we are. At times we may recognize ourselves as the elephant, and at other times we may identify with the trainer. When we compromise who we are in either situation, we live in a false relationship with ourselves. Our weakness rather than our power is showcased. If the elephant were aware of the ultimate consequences of its choices, it is doubtful it would choose to continue the journey to the circus ring. We have the opportunity to make that choice. To do so, we must develop an awareness of the consequences of our choices in order to change our destiny.

THE AUTHENTIC PEANUT

We Are Made to Live Authentically

At the deepest point of our being, there is an energy that identifies who we are as an individual. This energy is present within each of us, but the character of it distinguishes us from anyone else who has lived or is yet to live. It is in this energy that we are able to both define who we are as an individual person and discover the unique purpose that brings meaning to our life. The commonly used expression of the need to "find ourselves" describes our built-in need to not only connect with this force but also integrate it into our lives so that we can find direction or purpose. We do not create this need as such; it is simply how we are made. We can ignore it or reject it, but we cannot change or destroy it. This need cannot go away because it is an inherent part of who we are as human beings.

The need to find ourselves may surface at various times in our lives and in varying degrees. When it is not met, it can be detected within ourselves and can even be observed by others. It creates a kind of restlessness and a loss of focus or purpose. There is a sense that we are not living in sync with our potential. Most important, this is experienced as an unrelenting need that must be addressed in order to achieve, or return to, a kind of stability and peace within

1

us. This need can be described as a kind of plea from within ourselves to either find or retrieve the power that gives shape to our authentic person. We have the freedom to decide whether we wish to address this need. As with any choice, there are consequences attached to our decision. If we choose to pursue the connection to our inner power in the way we live, we become more integrated or genuine persons. Therefore, for the purposes of this discussion, such choices will be described as Authentic Peanuts. On the other hand, the choices that ignore this pursuit will be termed False Peanuts because they disconnect us from our inner self.

Authentic Peanuts

The ultimate purpose of Authentic Peanuts is to enable us to be in possession of the power within us that uniquely defines who we are and our purpose in life. When people are able to tap into this sense of who they are, such occurrences are frequently described as defining moments. Our strengths surface and we are given a new sense of direction and purpose. These experiences not only tell us what we can do but also connect us to a source of energy that can make it happen. They occur under all kinds of circumstances. Some people experience such moments at a time of crisis. The result is a kind of value clarification for them. Others experience them at more tranquil moments, for example, while reading a book, watching a movie, or witnessing a friend go through the same process. Still others experience them when they are exposed to an opportunity and immediately know that it is something they must do. Whatever the circumstances, defining experiences are positive and dynamic occasions that liberate our spirits and focus our energies. They free us from the tensions of indecision and doubt and lead us to a sense of purpose and direction. We experience them as a kind of driving force in our lives that both defines and unleashes the energies of our spirit and gives us the determination to make it a part of how we will live. They are integrating experiences because they enable us to not only define our power but honor it in our choices. People who are successful at this type of integration are frequently described as "having it together." The experiences provide a kind of peace and confidence in who we are. And because we are not under the pressure of pretense, there is a natural flow of our energy rather than a restraint of it. It is comfortable to be in the company of people who have done this because they don't have an agenda. Such persons have a sense of self-possession. They inspire because they have the courage to express the very soul of who they are in what they do and say. Finally, this provides a sense of stability and security within because we are living out of the anchor of our own convictions rather than accommodating to perceived externally imposed expectations.

Defining moments are intensely personal. No one else can write the script for us. Others may be able to observe when we have or have not connected to the process, but they cannot tell us what it should be. At times this is difficult, especially for parents who desire the best for their children and attempt to lead them into a particular career or relationship. But doing so not only imposes an artificial sense of power on another; it is also an invalid expression of one's own power. We can neither design the power within ourselves nor design it in another. To attempt to externally impose talents, gifts, or characteristics creates an internal division that cripples rather than encourages the expression of one's purpose. The following actual experiences illustrate the effect on both parties involved when such impositions are attempted.

A successful sculptor shared that his parents discouraged him from pursuing an artistic career in favor of a more materially successful business career such as they had experienced. Initially he accommodated their request, but that did not take away the desire within him. It only suppressed it until he was able to free himself from the artificial restraint that his parents placed upon the expression of his gifts as a sculptor. In this internal freedom he found and followed his purpose.

Another man shared that he felt his heart attack was related to the stress he experienced when his son decided not to follow the business career that he had planned for him. The man believed he could and should provide for a successful future for his son. But this was an invalid premise. His son's desire was to be an auto mechanic. Whether or not this contributed to his illness, the fact remains that the father's false sense of power for his son was confronted and created a serious internal conflict for him.

We can only be responsible for the power within ourselves. The more we are in possession of our own power, the less likely we are to attempt to impose power on another.

False Peanuts

False Peanuts could also be termed inauthentic or disintegrating peanuts because they consist of choices that *betray the spirit within us*. They *depersonalize* us by either denying who we are or refusing to acknowledge it in the way we live.

False Peanuts may prompt us to take on characteristics that are not our own. However, we seldom choose such behavior just for the sake of pretense. Our motives more often are to make ourselves look better so we will be accepted or fit in. At other times we may select a False Peanut because we think it will make someone else happy. We then become like the elephant who sacrifices itself in order to please the crowd. Unfortunately, at times the expectations we think others have of us may not even be real, but the consequence for us is the same.

False Peanuts can likewise be found in the use of external circumstances to define our person. This is frequently observed in such socioeconomic factors as the car we drive, the house we own, the labels we wear, the school at which we were educated, the job we have, and our family background. If we do not have a strong personal identity, we are more likely to use the crutch of an external circumstance to define who we are. A friend related the story of a mutual acquaintance who was a retired CEO. Years after his retirement, he continued to introduce himself as a "has-been CEO." It would seem that a part of his identity was still tied to a circumstance of the past. To engage in such behavior sends a subtle message of identity based on position, which is an invalid premise for personal identity.

On the other hand, Christopher Reeve exemplified the value of establishing one's identity within himself. He was very successful as an actor. For many of us his identity was tied to his role as Superman. A tragic accident ended his acting career. However, it was in this set of circumstances that he demonstrated to us that his person was more than who he was as an actor. He demonstrated an incredible personal strength that enabled him to pursue a meaningful life in a severely incapacitated state. In fact, it would appear that we learned more about Reeve as a person after his accident than we did in his role as an actor. He clearly had not established his personal identity on his ability to perform for or please the crowds.

Lance Armstrong also had the courage to acknowledge this issue within himself when he was diagnosed with cancer. In his book *It's Not About the Bike: My Journey Back to Life,* he states, "I realized it [cancer] wouldn't just derail my career, it would deprive me of my entire definition of who I was...Who would I be if I wasn't Lance Armstrong, world-class cyclist?"

Ultimately False Peanuts betray and deny our authentic power. They are transient, arbitrary, inauthentic, and disintegrating forces in the process of self-definition. They prompt us to sell our souls to please the crowd. The result is a kind of human domestication process that conditions us to respond to the commands of others at the risk of never knowing who we truly are. The rewards are false because the peanuts are false. Therefore, they always leave us with a kind of emptiness and the sense of searching for something more. They may pacify but will never satisfy our inner longings. In fact, they may engender negative feelings such as resentment or jealousy. The multiple roles that many of us have today can compound this situation. We can at one and the same time be child, parent, spouse, friend, employee, and boss, all with specific expectations. We can easily feel torn apart by the demands and expectations of our many roles unless we are living out of a consistent core within ourselves.

The fact that we are made to live in an authentic way is not just an intellectual theory. It is something real in our lives, and there are clear signals that tell us when we are or are not living in this way. Lie detector tests indicate that even our bodies react to deceit. We can accept and appreciate differences among people, but we find it difficult to accept people who act like someone they are not. We can detect phony behavior. We mistrust and reject it. It makes us uncomfortable even when we are not deeply involved. It reflects the innate need we have for authenticity in others as well as in ourselves.

The job of the Authentic Peanut is to enable us to make the choices that empower us to be who we truly are. This involves an emptying out of who we are *not* as well as discovering who we *are*. It involves peeling off the layers of perceived expectations of who we *should* be in order to free the spirit that is within us. If the elephant had rejected the external expectations imposed by the trainer, it never would have ended up in the circus. Authentic Peanuts always result in an integration of *who we are* with *how we live*. They move us outside the trained behavior that is showcased in the performance ring of the circus.

THE FREEDOM PEANUT

*Freedom Is the Ability to Choose to
Act on the Power within Ourselves*

We live in a society that is very conscious of the need for freedom. Demonstrations supporting specific causes are commonplace because of the perception that our freedoms are at risk. While such demonstrations may support valid causes, they can also be misleading representations of true freedom.

The first problem is that these issues present a kind of relative freedom. What makes one person feel free may make another person feel oppressed. The issue of freedom of religion in the United States is an example of this conflict. One group feels that freedom of religion should mean the ability to express one's religion in public. Another group feels that the expression of religion in public is an imposition on the freedom of those who do not believe in religion. Such freedom is subjective or relative because it depends on personal viewpoints.

The second problem is that this kind of freedom is issue based. As one issue is resolved, another surfaces. Since we will never run out of issues, our freedom is limited to the extent that it is related to such issues.

A third concern with issue-based freedom is that it hinges on rights of ours over which someone else has control. So our freedom becomes dependent on a source outside ourselves.

And finally, if freedom is based on the absence of circumstances, such as the absence of religious statues in public places, it becomes a negative—an absence of something rather than a presence of something.

We can logically conclude, therefore, that if we choose to define freedom as related to causes or circumstances, we are defining a limited concept of freedom. Such freedom is not consistent with the deeper experiences of freedom expressed by Holocaust survivors such as Viktor Frankl. We are well aware of the terrible oppressions to which these people were subjected, but, in spite of this, they were still able to obtain a freedom of spirit within themselves. Their lives teach us that personal freedom is not dependent on external circumstances. Freedom is about choice and personal control. It is a quality that resides within ourselves. It is a power from within that liberates us to be our own person.

It would seem, then, that although there are certainly unjust situations in life that we should make every effort to correct, we should not confuse these issues with true personal freedom. We would do ourselves an injustice if we allowed our freedom to be dictated by the presence or absence of circumstances, some of which may be in the control of others. In fact, it would connote a very limiting notion of freedom that would restrict rather than free. It would suggest that freedom is based on a formula of external events. If we were fortunate enough to fit into a favorable formula, we would be free. This concept of freedom is passive. It gives the responsibility to someone else and views it as a matter that is out of our hands.

We live in the midst of circumstances. Some are positive and some are challenging. There are profound and inspiring accounts of people who have found themselves in the midst of adversity. They were pushed to go deeper than the external situation and tap into an inner strength that defined them in a whole new way. In the exercise of this internal freedom, they defined themselves. They realized that their strength went far beyond the situation at hand. These individuals teach us that freedom is a deeply personal and dynamic concept, that it enables us to break free of circumstances in order to uniquely define who we are, and that it both inspires and energizes because it gives definition to our spirit. Freedom is what shapes us as a person.

The choices of such freedom are the most important of our lives because they offer us the opportunity to give voice to the power within ourselves. A physician once shared with me that he had requested orders to go to Vietnam because he believed it would be an opportunity to find out who he really was. In a sense he was saying that he knew who he was in the midst of comfortable American circumstances, but he wanted to know who he would be when these circumstances were removed and replaced by the physical and psychological stresses of war. Essentially he was searching for what he was made of regardless of circumstances. This is a classic illustration of the search for personal freedom. In the midst of circumstances that would seem restrictive to many of us, he saw an opportunity to identify his true self. This is not an isolated example. The same could be said of many men and women who volunteer for military service or accept public service jobs that endanger their lives. They accept the risk of war and conflict because of their conviction that in some way the experience will enrich their lives at a deeper level.

In the midst of such experiences, people seem to discover a resource within themselves that they never knew existed and might not ever have known were it not for a crisis. These experiences show us that personal freedom is dynamic. It is not something that passively resides within us but is an energy that needs to be surfaced and exercised. There are many things we may wish to be or do, but it is not until we exercise our personal freedom to act on these wishes that we will define our spirit. We might say that freedom is a potential within us until it is acted upon, that it waits for us to choose it. The Freedom Peanut urges us to choose to act on the powers within ourselves and discover our potential. It is in this process that our true self is liberated—it is no longer dependent on external factors that we once thought were essential to defining us.

When we define freedom by external circumstances, we encounter the risk of developing a victim mentality. This encourages us to use the "if" theory. We may admit we are a certain type of person but readily add that "if circumstances were different," we could be a different and better person. But this is not valid. We can live in a society that is free but still not be free within ourselves, and we can be free while living in an oppressive society. It is clear that in the "if" theory, we abdicate personal responsibility for who we are, which robs us of the freedom we have been given in life to claim and give shape to ourselves. All of us have heard of people who rose out of incredibly limiting circumstances to define themselves and prove that those circumstances were not the defining criteria of who they were. Their courage enabled them to liberate the force that was held captive within themselves and therefore conquer external circumstances.

The life of Martin Luther King Jr. clearly models the Freedom Peanut concept. He experienced the same external oppression as many of his brothers and sisters, but he refused to let his spirit be oppressed by these circumstances. The choices we make define the person we become. Unquestionably the choice that enriched the lives of millions of others also enriched King's own life. He could have chosen otherwise. But he refused to hand his person over to the circumstances of oppression. He chose instead to lead the freedom movement that changed history. If he had chosen oppression, we would never know him as the man we know today. He became effective in the cause of freedom because he was a free man—not free from oppression but free to shape and define his own person because he acknowledged and tapped into the power within himself.

Each of us experiences some kind of oppression in our lives, perhaps in a relationship, a job, a physical condition, or a social issue. We all have the ability in our own way to follow the example of Martin Luther King Jr. We can reach within ourselves and discover the resources we possess to empower us to handle our challenges, or we can choose to be victims by handing over our power to the circumstances that will dictate who we become. If we choose to accept the peanuts of circumstance, we risk never really knowing our true potential. This route may be more comfortable since we can always console ourselves with the fact that the problem is in our surroundings and not within ourselves. But then we must also recognize the fact that we *choose* to compromise the integrity of who we are by letting circumstances define us. We need to realize that the surrender of ourselves to external circumstances cripples our personal freedom.

The Freedom Peanut gives us the ability to rise above and beyond circumstances. It tells us that circumstances can never validly define who we are. We can live in a free society and still not be free within ourselves, or we can live in an oppressed environment and be free within. To the extent that we are truly free within ourselves, we will also be free from using others to define who we are. A liberating and life-giving force will be apparent for both ourselves and those with whom we relate. This may be the deepest task of our lives and also the most meaningful. Using our Freedom Peanut places the power of our lives in our own hands. It releases us from the bondage that inhibits the expression of our personal power.

In his book *Man's Search for Meaning*, Viktor Frankl states, "Everything can be taken from man but one thing: the last of the human freedoms—to choose one's own attitudes in any given set of circumstances, to choose one's own way."

THE COURAGE PEANUT

*Courage Is the Ability to
Challenge the Fear in Oneself*

I n *The Wizard of Oz*, the lion requested that the wizard give him courage to overcome his fear. The lion knew he was a lion, but he also knew that his fear was an obstacle to living as a lion should live. Fear was the cause as well as the symptom of the lion's distress. In granting the lion's request, the wizard simply told him, "All you need is confidence in yourself."

The response of the wizard was startling indeed. After a long and arduous journey in search of the person who could give him courage, the lion was told the answer was within himself all along. The wizard could not give him the courage he sought; he had to do that for himself. And clearly the point that was made for the lion is the point that was made for us. We tend to project the causes of our fears as outside of ourselves, and therefore the solutions to our fears are likewise outside of ourselves. We are generally quite comfortable expressing the objects of our fear—the dark, airplanes, enclosed spaces, and so forth. Frequently there is even a kind of self-acceptance regarding these fears, with little motivation to change. It becomes a matter of simply avoiding those situations rather than addressing the source of our fears, which is inside of ourselves. We perceive a risk, a potential danger to ourselves, but are unwilling to give ourselves the opportunity to overcome this fear. Our fear paralyzes our potential. We continue to be controlled by the possibilities that the object of our fear holds. Fear prevents us from taking the risk to find out if in fact harm will actually be inflicted. We permit our fears to define who we will be. Courage, on the other hand, is the ability to challenge the fear within in order to release ourselves from the control it has over us. It is a willingness to confront fear rather than accept it in order to unveil our true potential. The following account illustrates the significant impact that can occur in an individual's life when the risk is taken to challenge one's fears.

A young man felt confident that he had a calling to the priesthood. He followed the usual procedures for application and was pleased to be accepted for entrance into the seminary. After a period of time, however, an advisor suggested that, because of his unsatisfactory grades, he should consider the possibility that this was not his vocation. He chose to remain in the seminary even though his grades placed him third lowest in the class. On his first assignment, he was still troubled by the advisor's assessment of his abilities, so he decided to enroll in a community college course to test his academic abilities. In order to minimize his perceived risks, he chose not to share with anyone else that he was taking the course. He enjoyed the course and received an A, which gave him the courage to enroll in a second and then a third course, both of which also resulted in As. Encouraged by this experience, he eventually went on to earn a doctorate degree and subsequently published several books.

This experience illustrates the fact that fear can rob us of the opportunity to discover the truth about our own potential. Fear is the easy way out because it excuses us from both knowing and using our potential. Had this man not taken the risks involved to overcome his fear, he would never have known his true potential and would have lived according to someone else's perception of who he was. His courage enabled him to take possession of who he was rather than permit a force outside himself to dictate who he was. His courage removed the roadblocks that were within him.

However, his story could have ended differently; the advisor's assessment could have been accurate. But this still would not have been a failure because the risk would have enabled him to determine for himself what his abilities were and what they were not. He still would have been able to claim for himself his own true potential. The ultimate quest of courage is to know the truth of who we are and who we are not, which raises self-confidence and removes fear. Risk implies an unknown. Without risk we cannot determine our full potential.

Another significant aspect of this man's story relates to the judgment that another person made of his ability. His life would have been significantly different if he had simply accepted the advice of his advisor and did not accept the responsibility for determining his own capabilities, and he could have blamed this on the advisor. Blame is the deathblow to courage, as it removes both the opportunity to develop confidence in oneself and the responsibility to do so. Self-confidence can only come from within, and self-confidence is the only cure for fear. Another person may facilitate self-confidence, but only we can acquire it for ourselves.

Courage is frequently associated with high-profile events. But courage seldom makes such an appearance without preparation. Athletes who win in competitive events have repeatedly practiced courage in the challenges they accepted during their training. Captain Chesley "Sully" Sullenberger, who exemplified great courage while safely landing a plane on the Hudson River, likewise had exercised courage in many flights prior to that experience. We may anticipate legitimate fears, such as handling the death of a loved one or losing our job, but the way in which we handle these difficult situations will be built on the courage we exhibit in our daily lives. Confidence in oneself is an ongoing journey because we are continually faced with new challenges that shape our self-confidence.

If courage is to lead us on the path to self-fulfillment, it must require us to live according to our values. It is not a candy-store approach in which we simply select what appears on the surface to be the most satisfying. Courage must be connected to our underlying values or it is self-defeating and disintegrating. At times it is precisely the values we hold that create a risk. On occasion people in high-profile positions have decided to resign knowing full well the risks involved in losing such a good salary or benefits; they are willing to risk this because what they are doing in this position is not connecting with the values they hold. Courage is not for the faint-hearted because it does involve risk. However, unless the risks are clearly defined, what appears to be courage may actually be weakness. People who steal risk the chance of being caught and punished. Such risk cannot be termed courage because it is not value driven. The courage that enhances our person is determined by what we fear and what we are willing to risk.

Perhaps the most popular statement of Franklin Delano Roosevelt's presidency was "The only thing we have to fear is fear itself." The most fatal fear is the fear to try. Such fear creates a false sense of security because it makes us feel safe in what we are doing but never tells us what more we are capable of doing. Courage mobilizes our energies and transforms potential into reality. Courage opens the very doors of the soul and imprints our spirit on what we do. It allows us to love even when we are not loved in return, to forgive even when we are not forgiven, to respect and understand even when we are not respected or understood. With courage, we are able to maintain our values in the face of unknown risks, and we can identify opportunities that others may view as obstacles. Courage removes the crutches that we unconsciously develop to protect ourselves from addressing the very fears that inhibit us. It removes the limitations on what we will do because it is grounded in confidence in oneself.

THE LOYALTY PEANUT

PEANUT PRINCIPLE

4

Loyalty Is Faithfulness without Bondage

L oyalty is generally perceived as an expression of faithfulness and caring toward another person, cause, or organization. It is more than a passing emotion or intellectual concept because it is translated into what we *do*. It is intensely personal and serves as a kind of window that enables us to see what is within the heart of a person. Loyalty is unwavering in expressing its faithfulness even when externally its purpose may seem questionable. Rabbi Harold S. Kushner relates an example of such faithfulness in his book *Overcoming Life's Disappointments*. He speaks of a man who continued daily visits to his wife who was afflicted with Alzheimer's disease even though she was unable to recognize him. In response to the question of why he continued to do this, he said, "She may not know who I am. But I know who I am." It was the need to express his love and faithfulness to her that motivated his visits.

The expression of such loyalty can also be seen in the rituals of organizations. The ceremonies that honor a fallen comrade in military or public service are particularly moving because they are inspired by both a commitment to a common cause as well as a bond of caring among one other. We cherish those moments when we either experience loyalty from others or express our genuine care to others because loyalty seems to reach within and touch the very souls of those involved.

However, loyalty is also a very fragile peanut. It is not uncommon for it to take a detour. In an effort to express our faithfulness to another, we can unintentionally take on their perceived expectations at the price of suffocating our own self. We can become robotic and program ourselves to do what we think will be pleasing to the other. But the object of loyalty is to authentically express *who we are* for another and, therefore, must be anchored in faithfulness to ourselves. Such faithfulness is the very core of loyalty. If it does not exist, we live out of a false relationship with who we are. We become slaves to someone else's expectations, which results in a disintegration of who we are. And it can all occur under the guise of being loyal.

A woman shared her experience of the consequences of such misguided loyalty in her marriage. When she married, she attempted to be a good wife and both learn and live the preferences of her husband. After a number of years the relationship failed. But it was not until after the separation that she began to realize how she took on his preferences, rather than her own, in the way she lived. She became an embodiment of who he was by choosing the clothes he liked, the entertainment he liked, and so on. In her effort to be loyal to him, she lost her own life and the relationship grew into a false one that failed.

Clearly there is a place for accommodation in relationships. But when accommodation is understood as conformity and mistaken for loyalty, the relationship is no longer built on respect for either party. Such behavior is more correctly described as "people pleasing." Under this misguided sense of loyalty we then assume the same consequences as the circus elephant. In the course of the conditioning process, the ultimate goal is to *use* the elephant to please *the audience*. The elephant is judged faithful to the extent that it cooperates in performing this way. It is clear that in this process the elephant loses the sense of faithfulness to its true self. But what can be said of the audience who sets and accepts expectations for entertainment that are contrary to the integrity of the elephant? It would seem that the circus elephant tells us as much about the audience as it does about the elephant. Both are compromised because loyalty neither accepts nor imposes actions that diminish integrity. To impose them is manipulation, and to accept them is to be a victim.

It is important to recognize this dynamic because each time we permit the power of another to dominate or direct our behavior, we become victim. We become tied to what another wants and lose control of our own power. Such misguided loyalty leads to abuse. The greater the loyalty attached to the relationship, the more difficult it is to acknowledge and disclose the abuse. It may be either physical or psychological abuse. Surely this would be the case in domestic abuse where the consequences of disclosing parental or spousal abuse could appear to be disloyal. Just as difficult is the disclosure of abuse within religious, professional, or social organizations. The preconceived convictions of loyalty are intimidating factors in disclosing abusive behavior. However, to refrain from disclosure is not faithfulness to ourselves or to the abuser because it continues to hold truth in bondage and the persons involved as victims. No organization, relationship, or position can justify abuse under the guise of loyalty.

Because loyalty involves caring, it is sometimes clouded by the emotion attached to certain experiences. This is true especially at the death of a loved one. A friend shared her experience regarding this when she was handling the grieving process after her husband's death. They enjoyed a great relationship, and she sincerely missed him. But as she progressed in processing her grief and began to experience some happiness again, she also felt guilty. She thought it was not loyal to him to be able to experience happiness again without him. But this is an invalid formula. It suggests that if we were happy with one person in the past, we should never be happy again unless that person is present. To accept this creates a victim mentality because our happiness is placed in the hands of circumstances over which we have no control. It puts the rest of our life on hold because it ties us to a past relationship. Our energies are suppressed because of our partner's death. If we accept this we are faithful to neither ourselves nor our loved one. In binding ourselves to the imagined energies of the person who can no longer speak for himself, we create a kind of bondage that paralyzes our own energies. Of course this woman continues to love and miss her husband. But once she was able to drop the guilt of being happy, she was able to legitimately remove the bondage she placed on her own spirit.

At times children who are involved in the grieving process take on this dynamic for their surviving parent. They not only believe a surviving parent cannot experience happiness without the deceased parent, but they further believe that, out of a sense of loyalty, the surviving parent should not even attempt to be happy with another spouse. A child may continue to validly hold loving feelings for the deceased parent. But it is invalid to impose criteria of loyalty that ask a surviving parent to continue to live under the shadow of what happened to their partner. Loyalty is of the heart, and we cannot define what is or should be in the heart of another. When we do attempt to define what another should or should not do, it is more often a projection of our own internal conflict. When we are able to reconcile within ourselves, we are more likely to free others to embrace the reality of the current circumstances in their own lives. The emotional component that is involved in the death of a loved one is difficult to objectify. But if we are not willing to confront the invalid basis for our loyalty, we keep ourselves chained to the past, which cripples the present.

The object of our loyalty is not confined to interpersonal relationships. Because it involves faithfulness, it can be extended to any arena in which we have invested our energies. Our workplace is one such area and is often a controversial object of loyalty. It is not at all uncommon to hear such expressions as "Loyalty doesn't count anymore" or "I will never be loyal to a company again after what I saw happen to my father." The reference, of course, is to the fact that downsizing occurred. It is certainly a very emotional experience to lose one's job. But this connection to loyalty bears further consideration. Few, if any, employment agreements include a clause stipulating that employment is permanent. But even if all legitimate contract agreements have been met, when downsizing is necessary it is frequently viewed as a lack of loyalty on the part of the employer. It further creates a sense of having been victimized and leads to the determination, therefore, that one will never be loyal to an employer again. If we believe that loyalty is faithfulness to what is within oneself and that how we performed was consistent with that, it appears invalid to project the consequences for our future performance on the disloyalty of the employer. If we worked extra hours, was it to satisfy our own sense of fulfillment, or was it done with the false expectation that it would guarantee permanent employment regardless of current economic conditions? This is certainly not intended to downplay the psychological difficulties of losing one's job. It is simply an attempt to dissect the concept of loyalty and therefore eliminate consequences that are potentially detrimental to oneself. The bondage that held us to our loyalty in the past may have been a false bondage of entitlement. We may determine never to be loyal again based on false premises that have the potential to diminish who we are.

In spite of many of our current cultural conditions that discourage a sense of loyalty, we need to recognize the value of loyalty for our own integrity. The Loyalty Peanut suggests that loyalty is faithfulness to our own spirit without bondage to external expectations. If we cannot free ourselves to care and give of ourselves because of real or imagined risks, we have become victims, enslaved by those risks. If we no longer care enough to commit ourselves to a person, job, or cause, we have lost the spirit that gives life to our souls. We have reduced our lives to a mere formula that fractures the truth within us. Although it is possible to live in this way, it is self-defeating. The Loyalty Peanut can release us from such bondage and enable us to own our spirit as we are confronted with the decisions that are a part of our daily lives.

THE FORGIVENESS PEANUT

Forgiveness Is Freeing Ourselves from the Power of Another's Actions

There is no peanut that is more common to all of us and yet more perplexing than the Forgiveness Peanut. The need to forgive and to be forgiven is a universal experience. It has been a part of every age in every culture. Not a single one of us escapes the need to forgive and to be forgiven. It is a part of our human condition. But in spite of this ever-present need and the numerous books, advice columnists, and even religious leaders suggesting how to forgive, our understanding of forgiveness frequently still lacks clarity. One of the most common definitions of forgiveness is "to forgive is to forget," which would suggest that the primary dynamic at play is forgetting. Another popular maxim from the movie *Love Story* concludes that "love means never having to say you're sorry." Does this mean that saying "I'm sorry" is the primary factor in forgiveness? Even some traditional religious practices present questions. Do religions that embrace a form of confession have an edge on forgiveness? Does forgiveness by God mean forgiveness among the people involved? Of further interest is the fact that in the Lord's Prayer, millions of people throughout the world repeatedly ask to be forgiven as we forgive. In view of all of this ambiguity regarding the definition of forgiveness, how then do we define what it is that we seek?

All of these concepts of forgiveness certainly offer some value in addressing the ultimate objective of forgiveness, which is to somehow reconcile the consequences of a wrongdoing. However, for many of us the focus in forgiveness is primarily on the person *wronged* and overlooks the consequences for the person who *performed* the wrongdoing. To do this is to address only part of the process because clearly when we do wrong to another, we also do wrong to ourselves. The two cannot be separated. It is not a matter of two choices; there are simply two consequences of the same act. In some circumstances, when we have wronged another, we may feel we have gotten away with something. We may steal, cheat, lie, or abuse, and no one seems to notice. Externally that may be true, but we cannot escape the internal consequences. We become the peanuts we eat. When we do wrong to another, it affects the person we are regardless of whether anyone else knows what we did or did not do. A lack of acknowledgment by anyone outside ourselves does not affect the fact that we have violated our own personal integrity.

To focus, therefore, only on what happened to the person harmed creates an invalid expectation concerning forgiveness. This is only one aspect to be considered. Forgiveness is not, and cannot be, a magic button God or anyone else can push that will mysteriously relieve us of our responsibility for having done wrong and make everything okay again. Forgiveness must be a process involving the person who *has* wronged as well as the person who *was* wronged.

Forgiveness of Self

In order to forgive ourselves of a wrong, we need to first recognize and assume responsibility for the wrong committed. We all make mistakes, are sorry for them, and need to correct them. If we cannot truthfully acknowledge we were wrong, we cannot correct it. It remains within us but is unresolved and divides the integrity of who we are. On the other hand, if we acknowledge it but refuse to forgive ourselves or let go of it, it restricts us. We define ourselves by what we *did* rather than by what we *can do*. We establish a kind of bondage to a peanut of the past and continue to let that define who we are. The point of forgiving is to free us of this bondage.

Two of the disciples of Jesus betrayed him. Judas agreed to identify Jesus to those who were seeking to arrest and kill him. After he did this, however, he hung himself in despair. He knew he had done wrong but was not able to reconcile this within himself. Peter also betrayed Jesus by denying that he knew Him. However, it appears that he refused to let this denial become his entire identity as a person. In some way he was able to reconcile this wrong within himself and eventually became the leader of the church.

It is critical to reconcile misdeeds within oneself whether or not the external reconciliation with the person who was harmed ever occurs. Such reconciliation is clearly a related but separate issue. It is neither healthy nor valid to continue to bind ourselves in guilt because the one we have offended has chosen not to forgive. Forgiveness only by the person wronged does not translate into full forgiveness. This would make forgiveness a very arbitrary issue and would ignore the internal work required of the person who performed the wrong. It would mean that if we offended a kind person, we would more likely be forgiven. And conversely, if we offended an unforgiving person, our chances of being forgiven would be more unlikely. Our responsibility would be conditioned by the very subjective condition of *who* we offended rather than *what* we did. It would transfer the responsibility for righting the wrong to someone else. We could live in the traps of guilt for the rest of our lives because the other chose not to forgive. Or we could erroneously assume that we are forgiven even if we never did our own internal work regarding the incident. These clearly would be false conditions of forgiveness. We need to own what was done because we are the only ones who can recognize the cause of the wrong and reconcile this within ourselves, thus freeing ourselves of the associated guilt.

Forgiveness by the Person Harmed

The second aspect of forgiveness has to do with the person harmed in some way. One of the dictionary definitions of forgiveness is to "grant relief from payment." In other words, it means to take it off the books, to create a clean slate. This suggests that there is some kind of debt, that someone does *owe* us something. We need to free ourselves of this concept more for ourselves than for the other person. When we decide to hold onto a hurt and not forgive, we determine to build a little memorial within ourselves to be sure the hurt will never be forgotten. A part of us is dedicated to that. But as long as we do this, we claim ourselves as victims. Sometimes we speak of such situations as "eating away at a person" because they never are quite able to let go of what happened and reclaim their voice. But no one can claim us as victim without our permission. It is a matter of choice.

In attempting to let go of what another has done to us, we sometimes establish conditions as part of the forgiveness process. We can demand payment through an apology or some other standard of behavior before we will forgive. But in so doing we let someone else determine our freedom to forgive. There are many things we could say should legitimately happen in order to forgive someone. But as long as we hold onto these requirements, we place the control in someone else's hands. This is not intended to deny or make light of any wrong, nor is it meant to discourage making any appropriate amends. It is simply intended to help us identify the subtle pitfalls involved in the process of forgiving and being forgiven so we can heal.

A second element that is essential in forgiveness is the need to understand our own selves. We are well aware that on some days we are more susceptible to getting hurt than on others. One day someone can make a comment that will make us laugh and on another day the same comment can make us angry. Some years ago when I was having difficulty forgiving someone for a particular incident, I asked another person for their thoughts on forgiveness. The response was that I should understand and accept where I was at the time of the incident. At the time this answer seemed pretty vague to me. But after much thought, I concluded that the underlying suggestion was to understand what it was within myself that permitted me to be so vulnerable to what another did or said. Why did I permit someone else to have so much power over me through a real or perceived wrong? The image comes to mind of the piggyback games we played as children. Ultimately it was the person on my back that brought me down. When that extra baggage was removed, I could once again stand on my own and be free to move forward.

It is not uncommon for people to hold onto resentment for a lifetime. The message of what happened is continually re-sent. It's like living on constant replay. We may express it in such a way as choosing to never again speak to the person involved. But resentment, anger, or bitterness can never heal anything. In fact, the irony of such behavior is that we react to another's wrong by adopting behavior that does wrong to who we are. We diminish ourselves in order to get back at another. We begin to experience the same dynamic of the person who wronged us because, in failing to forgive, it is ourselves that we wrong. We may choose to do this for all kinds of reasons. We may do it as a kind of manipulation to impose guilt, to demonstrate to the other person just how wrong they were and how badly they hurt us. Or we may choose it as just payment. Regardless of the motive, we need to recognize that a lack of forgiveness, a lack of the ability to let go, ultimately impacts our own person. Forgiveness acknowledges that we are not responsible for what happened to us. We are only responsible for how we deal with it.

In summary, the Forgiveness Peanut reminds us that it is personally destructive to wrong another. But it is also personally destructive not to forgive a wrong, whether we commit it ourselves or it is us who are wronged. In either case, it is clear that we harm ourselves by holding onto the incident. To forgive is to become whole again. We reconcile or put ourselves together after having experienced that sense of being torn apart. It does not mean that we don't feel the pain and hurt of betrayal. It means that we refuse to let ourselves be diminished by the experience.

Such forgiveness does not mean that justice should not also be administered. There are clearly situations where our justice system should be exercised. But even then it should be recognized as an external process. Forgiveness, on the other hand, is an internal process. While the two may address the same issue, they are not the same. In fact, the two are exclusive of each other. Justice may be met without forgiveness. Forgiveness may be achieved without justice.

To forgive and be forgiven are two sides of the same coin. Our own personal integrity is at stake in both issues. This is not an easy process, particularly when injustice occurs. But to refuse to forgive or be forgiven holds us in bondage. We adopt a victim mentality that blames another instead of assuming responsibility for ourselves. We sometimes feel we do the other person a favor when we forgive. But the favor is really to ourselves. The Forgiveness Peanut tells us, as an anonymous quotation goes, that "to forgive is to set a prisoner free and to discover the prisoner is me."

THE POWER PEANUT

Our Power Can Only Be Validated within Ourselves

The desire to possess power is a normal human drive. It provides an important sense of direction and control. It enables us to own the consequences of our choices and prevents us from falling victim to external forces. However, power has many faces. If we do not have a clear concept of power, we can search for it in the wrong places and inadvertently become victims of a false power. True power is grounded in the internal spirit of our person and is reflected externally in what we do. It validates who we are as a person. False power, on the other hand, is driven by external forces and frequently contradicts and disintegrates the spirit that is within us. The following account illustrates how a person exercising such false power can in fact become more of a victim than the person over whom such power is exercised.

I had the good fortune of working with a woman who had been snatched from her family as a young teenager and placed in a concentration camp. I was intrigued by the fact that she was such a positive and kind person in spite of the horrible experiences she endured as a young woman. So one day I posed this question to her: how was she able to be so positive after having suffered such a negative experience? She indicated that in the beginning, the experiences of the camp were numbing. The abrupt transition to such traumatic conditions made it seem unreal. But as time went on, personal relationships developed and a very strong support system emerged among the prisoners and even among some of the guards. Those detained in the camp were obviously stripped of any kind of *external* power. But they demonstrated that their power was a force and an energy that was not dependent on external circumstances. The strength they shared was based on a power that was within them. They demonstrated that although we may not have the opportunity to choose our circumstances, we can choose how we respond to those circumstances. In fact, difficult circumstances can cause a power to surface that we did not even know we possessed. Furthermore, these circumstances can demonstrate that our power is, in fact, precisely *our* power. Nothing and no one outside of ourselves can either give it to us or take it from us.

On the other hand, Hitler, who had such obvious *external* power—the leader of a large and powerful army and the man who was in control of these persecutions—had established his power on false foundations. Instead of building his power from within, he established it on an arbitrary and external position of perceived power over others. As a consequence, when that position crumbled, his sense of power also crumbled and he ended up taking his own life. His suicide was the culmination of a death he had already experienced internally. His choices were directed to circumstances that weakened rather than strengthened his personal power. He had lost possession of himself before he lost possession of his life. Ultimately he demonstrated that our personal strength can never be found in the domination or destruction of others.

Although few of us will be subjected to these extreme circumstances, we are all vulnerable to becoming victims of such external power. The exercise of false power is not limited to heads of suffering nations. It can be identified throughout the civilized world in personal relationships as well as in political, professional, or religious organizations. False power is present whenever the *authority associ-*

ated with a position is misunderstood as *personal power.* Authority is restricted to a defined designation of the responsibilities associated with a particular position. It is external and limited in scope in so far as it is applicable only to the specific position. It does not and cannot bestow internal power on an individual. The amount of responsibility assigned to a position may define one's influence. But one is not more or less of a person because of the authority bestowed by the position. To attempt to define who we are by what we do is an injustice to ourselves because it reduces and restricts who we are to the narrow circumstances of a job. And when we depend on the position for our power, it is at the sacrifice of one's personal strength. Authority becomes a crutch and is exercised in a way that will meet the personal need to feel strong and in control. It is spurred on by personal weakness rather than strength. An intimidating style of management is frequently adopted to address the intimidation that is within. Because the outward control provides a sense of the inward control that is lacking, the inner drive for legitimate power is ignored. The position becomes an instrument of control over other people, generally without the insight that it is also controlling the individual who is exercising it. When we exercise authority with such rigidity, we are expressing the limitations of the weakness we have placed upon our own selves. When we search in the wrong places, we risk not ever knowing our true power because our true power is masked. We limit who we are by staying in a well-defined comfort zone. Positions are channels through which our personal energies are exercised; they are not an end in themselves.

The use of a position for personal agendas also encourages liberties for oneself that were never intended. This is undoubtedly the basis for many corporate scandals in which the perceived power of the position was used for personal purposes. An invalid sense of entitlement was attached to the position. But one cannot abuse one's position without abusing oneself. With the mask of power, however, those involved are among the last to recognize their weakness. They are among the last to realize that in abusing their positions, it is themselves they abuse. The abuse fragments the integrity of their power, and it is in this that they experience their personal demise.

When we seek our power in our position, it is invalid for ourselves as well as for those over whom we have authority. As we saw in the example of the young woman in the concentration camp, power cannot be imposed on another. Authority can be wielded over another, and often legitimately so, but it should not be confused with power over another. We may submit to externally imposed behaviors without surrendering our power. The story of Rosa Parks tells us that although our power may be subdued, it does not die. For years Rosa Parks accepted the imposition of the perceived power of segregationists that told her where she could sit on the bus. On the day that she refused to move to the "appropriate" seat, she said she was "just tired of giving in." The power within her was no longer willing to submit to the false power that was being imposed on her. In giving voice to her own power, Parks enabled millions of others to release the power that was pent up within them.

The purest theory may suggest that people control us only because we let them control us. While this theory may objectively be true, life is not always played out in objective terms. We are all in process. We all have an elephant element within us and at various times are more or less vulnerable to the domination of others. Perhaps immediate circumstances in our job or relationships may prevent us from either recognizing the dynamic or being able to remove ourselves from the situation. But the restlessness resulting from suppressed power will not go away until it is addressed. We could say that such restlessness is the refusal of our spirit to surrender.

The first step to regaining our personal power is to recognize that we have lost it. We are not sentenced to remain a victim; our power can always be retrieved. Although the abuser may remain blind to their misuse of power, the abused will always have the ability to *choose* to no longer sacrifice their spirit to the oppressor.

In summary, the Power Peanut tells us that the only legitimate power is that which is rooted within oneself. No one can give us that power or take it from us. When this power is abused, we violate the integrity of who we are. We become victim to our own selves when we search for the false power that is outside ourselves. In effect we lose the very power we are seeking.

THE CONNECTION PEANUT

Our Purpose Always Connects Us to Something Larger than Ourselves

There is an inherent desire within each of us to belong to something larger than ourselves. We experience a sense of satisfaction when we are able to do things that connect us with a greater whole. This is expressed in many of our day-to-day behaviors. We follow certain trends in clothing, eating, and entertainment that give us a feeling of being in sync with what others are doing. We enjoy wearing the team's colors at sporting events or meeting someone from our hometown. We join organizations that give us a sense of belonging to a shared purpose. All of these give us a sense of connection that is legitimate and enjoyable. But we are also keenly aware that these connections do not bring true, meaningful satisfaction. We can have all the latest trends and belong to all the right social organizations and yet still experience a sense of loneliness or isolation.

This desire for connection is grounded at a deeper level. It is the driving force that prompts us to extend ourselves to other people or causes in a way that results in a sense of personal fulfillment. It is the recognition that a larger force has already bound us together and that in some way we bear a responsibility for one another and are able to define our own purpose in helping one another. How else can we explain the heroic gestures of people who risk their lives to help people they have never met? How can we explain why Oskar Schindler risked his life to save thousands of Jews he did not even know from the gas chambers? The countless ways in which people reach out to others daily can only be explained because of a force that has somehow already bound us together. Such experiences suggest that we are all part of a larger whole. The Connection Peanut tells us that it is the part of the universe within each of us that not only draws us together but also clarifies our purpose as we define our responsibilities to the whole.

This force overrides the artificial separations we attempt to establish by such means as nationality, social status, or religion. In an interview with Anousheh Ansari after she flew to space as a tourist, she said, "The sheer beauty of it just brought tears to my eyes. If people could see Earth from up here, see it without those borders, see it without any differences in race or religion, they would have a completely different perspective. Because when you see it from that angle, you cannot think of your home or your country. All you can see is one Earth."

This force in which we participate makes no exception to the fact that each of us is given a distinct purpose that relates to the whole. We all share in the universe and are partners in shaping its future. Not all are asked to make high-profile contributions, but each has a place and contribution to make. In defining and fulfilling our specific purpose, not only are we fulfilled as individuals, but we affect the whole. The desire to fulfill our purpose or have an impact beyond ourselves is frequently expressed as wanting to make a difference or leaving the world a better place. It is the desire for our lives to have meaning. Meaning is found beyond an object or experience of itself. We keep mementos of trips and special occasions, knowing that they remind us of something bigger than the object itself. The meaning of the souvenir is found in its relationship to a larger event. So too with our lives—they are meaningful to the extent that we can connect them with something beyond our own life. When Martin Luther King Jr. was facing a prison term, he wrote the following to his wife: "I have the faith to believe that this excessive suffering that is now coming to our family will in some little way serve to make Atlanta a better city, Georgia a better state, and America a better country."

Larry Stewart was an anonymous Santa Claus who gave money to strangers for twenty-six years. When he revealed his identity, he said, "I see the smiles and looks of hopelessness turn to looks of hope in an instant. After all, isn't that what we were put here on Earth for—to help one another?"

The noted cellist Yo-Yo Ma expressed the belief that his music unites because it transcends such external differences as age, culture, and political views. He believes his music can make a difference and make the world a better place.

Our purpose is unique because it is directly related to who we are; when we identify and fulfill our purpose, it is a bridge to the rest of humanity. Even some people who live physically isolated lives have found meaningful ways to connect with others. These experiences reinforce the fact that a meaningful sense of belonging can transcend physical isolation.

The Connection Peanut is the ultimate integrator. It tells us that our sense of meaning and purpose is directly related to our ability to integrate who we are and what we do in order to integrate ourselves with the universe. This is a kind of paradox because as we more clearly define who we are, we come to realize that our purpose includes others. Our self-definition is never an end in itself; it is a means to participate in the greater whole.

Perhaps this larger vision was the driving force of people such as Pope John Paul II. His funeral was attended by the largest group of people on record. But the remarkable characteristic of the group was not the number of people as much as their composition. John Paul's death was mourned by people of various religions, ages, countries, political views, and walks of life. His death made it obvious that as he defined and carried out his task in life, he transcended the traditional cultural and religious barriers. He was connected with life at its deepest level, and he disregarded the boundaries and distinctions that can so easily justify our separation from the difficult or unappealing circumstances of others. The power this pope developed as a person was based on his sense of connection with all people and gave him a fearless determination to remove whatever obstacles oppressed the freedom of anyone. He recognized that at our deepest level we are one; his power was to reinforce this bond, not to isolate. Many news accounts described the occasion as "The world says goodbye to the pope." John Paul did not belong only to one church. He was a bridge to the disenfranchised wherever they were. He transformed the papacy into a global office and learned a dozen languages to reinforce the intent to connect as meaningfully as possible.

Princess Diana had a similar impact. Millions of people throughout the world mourned her death. But the reason they did so was not just that she was a part of the English royalty. People grieved because of what the "People's Princess" represented. In her life, Diana transcended the life of royalty and connected with the common experiences of the rest of humanity. Her causes reflected a concern for the underprivileged. Even her own personal experiences connected her to, rather than isolated her from, us. Princess Diana made herself one of us by extending herself beyond her royal position.

All of us are not called to this level of visibility. But we are called to a purpose. It is easier for us to believe that we may have made an impact on our family, our church, maybe even our city. But few of us would be comfortable believing we have contributed to the world, let alone the universe. In fact, it would be overwhelming for most of us to realize this. But the dictionary defines the universe as the "entire or whole." Earth is part of that whole and we are part of Earth. We share in the energy that comprises the universe. Each of us carries a part of the universe within us. The energy within us is no less a part of the total universe than anything or anyone else. We already belong to the universe. We are simply called to live in a way that recognizes this.

The sense of satisfaction that results from finding and making our contribution is unparalleled. It is invigorating, freeing, and peaceful. It is a sense of living out our purpose in life. As we reach out to contribute to the universe, we ourselves are changed in the process. It is as if we have found our place in the universe, and for many of us this is important before we can let go and die. It comforts us to know that the value of our life continues on in some way through what we have given or done for the cause of humanity. It is the realization that our energy comes from the universe and is destined to return to the universe through the way we live.

In summary, the Connection Peanut integrates us within ourselves and with the universe. It tells us that contributions do not belong only to the highly educated or powerful—they belong to each of us. It is not a question of whether we have a role, it is a question of what it is and if we are willing to commit to it. It requires us to drop all the excuses or insecurities that suggest that who we are or what we do really doesn't matter. The excuse of having nothing to contribute will be self-fulfilling and will rob us of the opportunity to fulfill our purpose. It may feel safer to refrain from acknowledging our real power or to hold that power under false cover. But the loss is to ourselves as well as to others. We risk not ever realizing the satisfaction of meaningfully connecting to others and will depend instead on external means that are arbitrary and transient. The Connection Peanut never seeks to dominate, divide, or control. It simply calls us to realize that we are already bonded with one another.

THE PERSISTENCE PEANUT

Persistence Transforms Potential into Purpose

Of all the peanuts, the Persistence Peanut has the potential to be the most challenging because it is unrelenting as it urges us to listen to the voice within. This voice not only tells us who we are but also suggests how high we can fly. Persistence is the driving force that enables us to transform our potential into our purpose. It is challenging because at times it seems to take hold of us more than we take hold of it. It becomes an imperative and we realize that what it suggests is something we have to do in order to be at peace within ourselves.

Persistence is grounded in the soul and is made visible in the choices we make. It invites us to walk into the unknown because it always calls us to be more than who we currently are. It is a dynamic force that pushes us forward to actualize the power within us, the power that defines our purpose. Because our purpose is rooted in who we are, it is accomplished whenever we live authentically. It is an expression of our spirit rather than the reason of our mind. Following this persistence may even require personal risk. It appears that persistence had hold of the man who held his ground during the historic confrontation at the Tiananmen Square pro-democracy protests. It was a force within that pushed him to step out from the crowd and stand up for a belief that he held in spite of the danger to his life. No one told him he was to do this; he knew within his soul that he had to. By validating the power that was within him, he also discovered his purpose.

The Persistence Peanut never calls us beyond what we can do, but it can suggest that we do what we previously thought impossible. When the Wright brothers entertained the idea that a machine could fly, persistence drove them to believe and accomplish what to that point had been impossible. They listened to the voice within that urged them to fulfill their specific purpose. The same could be said of many other inventors, such as Thomas Edison, who believed he could give us light with the flick of a switch. Edison could not let go of the idea that he could do what others had not accomplished.

By its nature, persistence is a creative force because it speaks in terms of possibilities. Persistence has inspired many people to overcome circumstances that initially appeared limiting. In Ohio, a young man without legs determined he could play football and did in fact become a successful member of his high school team. Marlee Matlin dared to believe that a deaf person could successfully hold a leading role in a motion picture. Such stories inspire because they tell of a spirit that refused to conform to perceived limitations. They listened to the voices of their souls and became so much greater than external perceptions deemed possible.

Our purpose is a journey rather than a specific destination. It is not lived out in single experiences but is ongoing. The following story demonstrates how single events can at times be the stepping-stones that lead us to our ultimate destiny. A motivational speaker read about a woman who lifted a car in order to release her grandson who was pinned beneath it. He was intrigued by the dynamics of such an experience and asked if he could visit with her. She agreed to a three-day visit, but whenever he approached the topic during the first two days of the visit, she cut him off. Finally, on the third day, he expressed his frustration and explained that he had flown across the country because she had agreed to share her experience.

The woman finally opened up and shared the fact that she was certainly very grateful that she was able to save her grandson. She had never dreamed that she had such power within her. But the reason she had been so reserved was that the situation had caused her to wonder what other untapped power she might have within her. The speaker then asked if there was any specific power this woman might have had that she regretted not using. She replied that she had always wanted to be a counselor for teens and had never done anything about it. Now she felt she was too old and she did not even have a high school education. In the course of the discussion that followed, she was able to remove the invalid barriers that had been preventing her from pursuing this dream. In time, she fulfilled all the necessary requirements and became a counselor for teens. The feat of lifting a car to save her grandson's life was an extraordinary accomplishment. But just as remarkable is the fact that it was the means to address an underlying desire she may never have fulfilled otherwise. Because of the incident, she was finally able to hear the voice of the Persistence Peanut that urged her to consider how she could achieve her purpose instead of the previous message of why she could not do so. To define our purpose and not be able to accomplish it is a contradiction; persistence always provides the tools to accomplish our purpose.

The experience of Lance Armstrong suggests that our purpose could be buried in the midst of adversity. He had a 3 percent chance of surviving cancer. After completing aggressive treatment, he reflected in his book *It's Not About the Bike*: "What if I had lost? What if I relapsed and the cancer came back? I still believe I would have gained something in the struggle, because in what time I had left I would have been a more complete, compassionate, and intelligent man, and therefore more alive. The one thing the illness has convinced me of beyond all doubt—more than any experience I've had as an athlete—is that we are much better than we know. We have unrealized capacities that sometimes only emerge in crisis." Each loss challenges us to transition to something bigger and deeper. It makes us less dependent on what we thought we could not do without. Persistence urges us to untie ourselves from the bonds that hold our energies captive. It is the belief that we hold the key to our power. Persistence never pretends to be the easiest path. It is just the most empowering path.

Henry Ford suggested, "One of the great discoveries a man makes, one of his great surprises, is to find that he can do what he was afraid he couldn't do. Most of the bars we beat against are in ourselves—we put them there, and we can take them down." Persistence is the force that will enable us to break down the barriers we carry within ourselves. Our inner self is the only force of enduring quality that can guide us on our journey. We can sabotage it or encourage it. Persistence will dictate our choice. It is the key that can set free the elephant within us and cut the ties that keep us victim to our own selves. It keeps us pushing when reason could tell us to stop. It accompanies us on the endless journey of transforming potential into power. And our potential is endless because the more we develop our power, the more capable we become of developing even more. In this process, persistence will continue to persist. It will not leave us until our purpose is fully accomplished.

EPILOGUE

In the Buddhist tradition, the elephant is associated with wisdom in the form of enlightenment. The elephant is at times seen as an adornment on shrines suggesting either an embodiment or protector of the sacred that is within the shrine. Some tribes even consumed parts of the elephant, believing they could thereby obtain some of its power for themselves. The most enduring and consistent role of the elephant has been associated with such symbols that represent a reverence for the power of the spirit within. But as is true with all symbols, they were not intended to represent the elephant itself. They were, and still are, meant to point to something beyond the elephant. These elephant symbols were intended to address the yearning to claim the power of the spirit within us. This elephant encompasses our power and purpose. It is the single most important possession we have. But it can be lost. It is lost or found in the choices we make. Claiming this power is not a simple task. In fact, it is a long process—a journey rather than a destination—as it is embedded in our everyday lives.

This process has been recognized and defined in various terms. Carl Jung calls it individuation. Joseph Campbell describes a similar process as defining your bliss. But what we choose to name it is not nearly as relevant as recognizing and addressing the issue for ourselves and within ourselves.

On occasion we hear of a kind of eruption of power within a domesticated elephant. There appears to be a kind of tsunamic force that wells up within it and results in a giant awakening of the futility of circus life. Even the trainer becomes aware that this emerging force within the elephant is no longer under its control. Somewhat like Rosa Parks, the elephant simply becomes tired of "giving in."

There is an energy within each of us that is unrelenting in its quest to express the uniqueness of who we are and to live this out as authentically as possible. This energy can be ignored, rejected, or repressed, but it can never be extinguished. It is the very core—the essence—of who we are as an individual. To connect with this energy is the single most important task of our lives. It is what gives us meaning, purpose, and fulfillment. Our choices will determine our destiny.

ABOUT THE AUTHOR

Aurelia's health care career provided rich opportunities to participate in a wide variety of life experiences. Starting as a registered nurse, she moved on to hospital education, pastoral care, and eventually received a master's in business that enabled her to work in hospital administration. She also served on various professional boards. After retiring from the health care setting, she assumed the position of pastoral administrator for her local church. She resides in Centerville, Ohio, with her husband, John. Please visit her website at www.aureliapalcher.com for more information.